The Retire

Preface

I often think back on a conversation I had with a close friend shortly after beginning my first semester in college. It was about 4 AM in the morning and we were sitting on the roof of my two-story townhome with a bottle of Jack Daniels, a pack of Marlboro Midnights, and a striking glass water pipe aptly named 'The Swan'. Amongst all our talk about the mysteries of life and the future, I asked a single question that changed the course of the entire conversation.

"So what do you want to do when you retire?" I asked.

"Retire? F*ck I work three jobs! I don't even know what my life's going to be like next month," replied Josue. He looked at me like I was a crazy madman on coke.

My life back then was a lot more carefree than it is right now. When I turned 18 I knew about the harshness of reality, I knew the downsides to adulthood; but no matter how big your ego is when you tackle the future, you only learn through experience. I wish I had known that back then. None the less, I still knew where I wanted to end up: it was the 'how' that I had to figure out.

"Alright your turn. What's your retirement plan?" retorted Josue.

"It's real simple. I don't know how it's going to happen, but the day I can afford a down payment on an apartment in Manhattan, that'll be the day that I retire."

It was destiny. For all the ambiguities and uncertainties that surrounded my life, I realized in that instant that throughout my life, the Manhattan goal was the one constant that kept me motivated to pull through all the obstacles that I had and would face.

"I guess that's pretty cool… what about after that?" asked Josue.

"Honestly, I just want to live out my days in a beach house either in Goa or Sicily. But I still got time to make up that decision so we'll see," I joked as I finished my cigarette.

"Well, good luck with that bro. I'm going to go back inside and pass the f*ck out somewhere," said Josue as he opened up my window and made his way back inside my room.

I stayed out for a few more minutes stargazing at the beautiful, winter, night sky. All I could think about from that day onwards was how I would make those drunken thoughts a reality.

Chapter 1: Passion & Warfare

Since day one, I had been immersed in the world of music and business. My parents had extensive backgrounds and experience in being over-qualified and under-paid. Hell, I remember doing their finances at the mere age of 11. On the other hand, my mother was a classically trained Hindustani singer and my dad had an incredible sense of rhythm and melody. Because of these two ingredients, I realized at a very early age my passion for music and everything about it.

Over the course of my pre-teen years, I found myself switching back and forth between piano and drums. I couldn't decide which instrument to pursue professionally until my freshman year in high school. Upon figuring out the first 10 seconds of Stairway to Heaven on the A string of a beat-up acoustic guitar, I decided that the guitar was the instrument that spoke to me the most.

After I moved back to America, I bought myself an electric guitar, and since then my life has not been the same. The electric guitar, to me, symbolized a realm of infinite sonic possibilities. I was obsessed with the shred metal movement and spent every insomnia-covered night practicing my technique and improvisational skills; on one of those nights, I found a guitarist that would really change my life: Steve Vai."

I remember learning his song, 'Tender Surrender,' in my first year on the guitar and instantly became ten times better at my craft, but also excited with what I could learn going forward, now completing that mammoth of a task. When I played that song, start to finish perfectly, for the first time ever I knew I wanted to be a musician.

My junior year, I began heavily involving myself within the musician cliques at my high school. I was regularly jamming with different bands, watching live shows on a weekly basis and playing any gig I could get my hands on; I slowly started to envision music being the career path that could potentially secure my future.

I decided that, with my business knowledge and expertise, combined with my ear for music, I could somehow string together an independent record label and start to use my connections to get me pointed in the right direction.

My heart was set on that idea. I signed up for a self-directed course and began studying and surveying the music business world. My goal in that course was that by the end of the semester I wanted to have a full-fledged plan for a record label that I could potentially start over the summer. I planned the entire semester; I covered it with different weekly projects and assignments that I swore to finish on my own outside of school.

For the first time in my life, I was organized and motivated to achieve my goals. I had 100 day plans, budget and break-even analyses, music store contacts, and even sales records for rappers that I worked with! I thought I had it all figured out - I could see my entire future becoming clearer and clearer day by day. In my head, I was thinking that I was going to drop out of school senior year and do this full time.

Unfortunately, my senior year didn't play out anything like that. My 'clients' outgrew their love for music and my carefree attitude found me on too many drugs and too depressed to care about music. The transition from spring to summer was a dark time for me, although, by my senior year, I developed a strange sense of comfort for those depressive mood swings. From the debacle that was my record label project, I still carried on my passion for music and business, this time with a new sense of maturity. I continued playing the guitar seriously and began focusing on getting myself together for college.

After graduating high school, I decided to take another crack at merging my love of music and business together, this time in the form of a custom guitar studio. This one proved to be more successful by far, as I found that by not anchoring my happiness on success, I could focus a lot more on the task at hand. A close friend of mine donated a $50 Squier Stratocaster guitar that looked like it had been run over by a tank, as a means of testing our skills on upgrading guitars.

By the end of the summer, my friend Sergio and I turned that beat up guitar into an $800 dollar guitar that looked nothing like it did when it first came limping to us. I was so proud of that accomplishment that I began investing my own money in the tools and equipment needed to carry out even more expensive upgrades, while also advertising my services as an uncertified luthier.

Now becoming a pattern, that plan too unfortunately had to stop. After an unfortunate falling out with my partner, I had to kill the shop and put all my faith into higher studies by readying myself up for college.

Chapter 2: Revelations

By the time college began, I had hair going past my shoulders, was seen always sporting black Levi jeans, and most importantly, partied on a regular basis. This chapter of my life begins on fateful evening when a couple of friends and I partied until 3 AM in the morning at my friend's house, Kristen, all the way in downtown Atlanta. My commute back home was a 25-mile drive, yet that distance had less of an impact shortly upon completing my first month of college. Anyhow, I had picked up Kristen from her barista job, where she would always fix me up my signature drink: 6 shots of espresso and mocha. What I didn't remember before mixing all my concoctions was that the next morning I had two entire essays due in two back-to-back classes.

Naturally, after coming down from my shenanigans around 2 AM and slowly remembering the two unfinished essays, I began to panic.

"Hon, don't worry, I got you covered! I still have your espresso in the kitchen. That should keep you up until you get home and finish your essay!" said Kristen, with the intent of comforting my anxiety.

"Dude, the coffee will barely get me through the first essay! I have two that need to be done. On top of that, it takes me half an hour to get home!" I replied.

She jokingly looked at me with a concerned look on her face - at least I thought she was joking. All hopes of finishing those essays started to diminish until Kristen said the one thing that changed the entire night.

"Hey, I ran out of creamer. The only thing that I have that will work is Bailey's. If you promise not to drink it until you get home, I can cream it with whiskey," she said, while screwing the top off the Bailey's bottle.

"Go for it. And you know me! I'll text you when I get home. Wish me luck."

After driving for thirty minutes, I finally reached my home with barely any energy to spare. I parked the car, grabbed the coffee cup sitting untouched in my cup holder, picked up my backpack, and ran to my bedroom.

I plugged in my laptop and hit the power switch. I could barely keep my eyes open as I watched the computer boot up so I decided to finish the entire mystery drink in one go. My computer turned on right after I was done and I was off like a horse on a racetrack.

The next morning I woke up beside my laptop with two files highlighted on my desktop. I immediately printed them out and rushed to college after getting ready. Without even going over the essays, I turned them in, satisfied solely based on the fact that I managed to get anything done, period.

To my surprise, I got back both essays a couple days later; each had a score that was no less than an 85!

Instantly, I began dialing Kristen's number to tell her the good news!

"Your drink worked! Holy f*ck it worked!" I exclaimed.

"You should be proud of yourself hon, the drink just let you do finish them more easily," she responded.

"Screw that. I'm calling that drink the KYOTS. It's the ultimate 'pick me up' drink," I said.

"Sure, you do that. Let me know if you ever need it again. I honestly didn't even think it would work out that well."

"You know what would be insane?" I asked, begging the question.

"What might that be?" she responded, biting the bait.

"A bar with this drink as its specialty drink. Nay! A bar by night and barista by day!" I answered, now brainstorming millions of variations for that concept.

I pitched this idea to my then new friend Josue, whom I met by chance while he worked at a local Pizza Hut.

By the end of the day, I had 20 tabs opened on my laptop browser regarding the KYOTS bar concept. I figured this may be the strongest chance I have at successfully utilizing my business and music expertise. The plan was to start one bar as a franchise with a live venue and baristas as partner franchises. From that point onwards, I saw Josue and I running the place together, and once we were to begin seeing profits, we would spread the bar around the country and let the franchise earn the money itself while we sat back and relaxed.

I remember the first time I pitched the idea to him as that night was one of my most favorite nights from my freshman year in college. It was Halloween night and my girlfriend and I had invited Josue and his girlfriend to go trick or treating with us. After we were done scavenging the rich country clubs of the vast Georgian suburbia, we retired to a local pub house, which, by then, had become a Halloween ritual altogether. Sitting there in our costumes, spirits high, we began ordering drinks and food.

After everyone was loaded up with enough drinks, we began to start connecting with each other even more. Our girlfriends switched seats to sit beside each other and immediately started clicking. My girlfriend was dressed in an ironic hipster getup that consisted of a denim jacket over a tank top complimented by John Lennon sunglasses. I, too, matched her with a hipster outfit of my own that consisted of a man-bun, black button down, galaxy themed suspenders, and of course, black Levi jeans. Josue and his girlfriend went as the Joker and Harley Quinn, based on the 2016 movie 'Suicide Squad'. Overall, those matchups made for some quite interesting pictures. But I digress.

Now watching the girls get along across the round table on the other side of the booth, Josue and I began our conversations. Overwhelmed by the excitement of this blossoming friendship, I decided to start bringing up KYOTS.

"If I realized anything tonight, it's that y'all are amazing people and I can't wait to see you guys at my wedding!" I joked.

"For sure dude! We just have to wait and see who f*cks up and gets married first," he responded.

"I don't know if you remember Kristen, but I have the craziest story from last Wednesday!" I said, trying to contain my excitement.

"The one from your college? Yeah, why?"

There was my in.

I proceeded to give him the rundown of KYOTS. After a solid five minutes of talking I paused, awaiting his initial response.

"Alright since we're starting to become closer, I'm going to tell you my biggest dream. I always wanted to start a bar in Costa Rica, back at home, and just open a bunch of those bars around the world. But, I also like your idea… so how about this, the day you manage to open the bar, I'm going to quit all my jobs and work there full time so that you can relax and focus on franchising?"

"We're going to get along just fine bro," I said, smiling uncontrollably.

Chapter 3: Treasure Hunters

My first year in college I was enlisted as a journalism major. Ever since I was a kid, the one passion that could potentially rival my passion for music was writing. I always loved watching the news and keeping up to date with what was going on in the world. And after reading about Forrest Fenn Josue and I had developed a thirst for adventure. I had reached a point in my life where the only times I felt true happiness was when I was away from current life back at home.

Normally, when people go public about their plans for a road trip, they tend to be swarmed by multiple loved ones - each with a single warning tale about the drive. Naturally, when Josue and I made the initial decision to drive cross country looking for treasure, we were instantly bombarded by precautionary tales from anyone who cared about our wellbeing and safety.

You guys might hit an animal!

Your car could break down in the middle of nowhere!

You might find yourselves having to live out of your car!

I hope you guys have enough money saved for cheap motels in the middle of nowhere!

Lord knows you guys love to have a good time. Try not to get arrested!

When people find the urge to share stories about their mishaps they usually center around one of the many things, if not more, mentioned above. Unfortunately for us, fortunate for you, if we were to have compiled a comprehensive list of every warning that was issued to us, by the end of the journey we may have very well crossed off most of the items. Regardless, we still went through with our plans and made sure the road trip happened.

The idea of the road trip was planted in our heads in January 2017. I happened upon an article detailing the death of a hiker who passed away searching for treasure in the Rockies. It was that hiker's one-year death anniversary. As a testament to true human nature, the single word from that article that stuck with me was: treasure.

After scavenging the vast world of the internet, I was directed towards a certain Mr. Forrest Fenn. As it happens, he had buried millions of dollars' worth of treasure somewhere in the Rockies, as described by a cryptic poem and detailed map of those mountains, located in various memoirs penned by him. For all I knew, the treasure still could have been out there. I called Josue and told him about my crazy plan to drive cross country and invited him to accompany me in March, if there was no news of anyone finding it by then.

He had the same idea. So, we both said screw it and began saving up for the adventure of a life time.

The deal we made was, if there was no news of the treasure being discovered by March of that year, we would try our luck at looking for it. The treasure's value was rumored to be anywhere between 1 to 5 million dollars; more than enough to make KYOTS a reality. With all my past attempts of making my dreams come true ending up huge failures, I figured we had a better shot at finding treasure in the Rockies than saving up and living the American dream by playing by the rules. Come March and there's still no updates on this nationwide treasure hunt, so as per the agreement, Josue and I quit our jobs and began packing up for the trip. Little did we know then just how much our lives would change over the course of the trip.

Chapter 4: Rocket Man

Josue

Amidst all the panicking and rain, Josue noticed the Prius was running low on gas. He drove to the nearest gas station past the Arkansas border, hoping to recuperate his thought, and figure out where to go from there. He remembered the last thing the state trooper said to him before driving off.

'If you guys had just been honest with us we would have let you off a lot easier.'

After driving for forty five minutes Josue managed to drag the Prius to a gas pump. He shuffled around in his pockets for a few minutes hoping to find any cash to pay for gas. He found Mihir's credit card in his wallet and used it to fill up a full tank, hoping to make it halfway home with that single fill up. After paying for the gas, he parked in front of the gas station's convenience store and began to figure out his next step.

After letting his girlfriend know what had happened in Oklahoma, he decided he should call Mihir's family and let them know what had happened. Upon looking for Mihir's father's number for fifteen minutes he made the call back to Mihir's home in Georgia. Mihir's father picked up.

"I got some bad news," said Josue, still fazed from the events that took place the hour before.

"Oh my God I was waiting for this call. Please tell me Mihir's ok!" responded Mihir's worried father.

"Mihir got arrested…"

"He got arrested? He got arrested! He got arrested!" exclaimed the father.

"I'm so sorry. Look tell me if there's anything I can do to help. I have all the information from the State Trooper with me. We still have $450 in the back seat and our credit cards. He's in Mayes county prison Oklahoma. I'm about an hour away from him. I was planning on bailing him out whenever they post bond," said Josue, trying to comfort Mihir's father.

"It's alright. I'll call the prison and see what's going on. You can go home. I'll take care of it," he responded.

Josue hung up the phone and decided to drive straight back home, since he felt like there wasn't much left that he could help with. As he merged back on the highway in the heavy rain, his girlfriend informed him of a huge storm covering the East coast all the way from Arkansas to Georgia. Josue couldn't help but feel stranded as the two week adventure came to a screeching halt that neither he nor Mihir were prepared for.

As word about Mihir's arrest spread, Josue began receiving phone calls from Mihir's family expressing their frustrations regarding Josue's freedom. Josue was mad at Mihir for taking the fall but, at the same time eternally grateful for Mihir's sacrifice, knowing what could've happened to him due to his already preexisting probation

16

sentence. As Josue continued to persevere through the dark and stormy roads, he only found comfort whilst listening to Rocket Man by Elton John paired with one of his Camel Crush cigarettes.

Josue drove through thunder and snow at full speed, and, against all odds, he managed to cure his homesickness by finding his way home safe and sound. The time at home was 1:30 AM and he barely finished unpacking his luggage. He walked into his house and kissed his girlfriend before lunging for his bed after the long drive.

"I missed you," said Josue, lying on top of his bedsheets and pillows.

"I missed you too!" replied his girlfriend.

"I missed you, bed," repeated Josue.

His girlfriend was left unamused, yet sympathetic. She left Josue to himself and went to take a shower. Within minutes, Josue was sound asleep.

Chapter 5: Start Me Up

After postponing our departure from nine thirty to twelve thirty, I finally managed to cross everything off my survival checklist whilst simultaneously fitting all my luggage into the compact Prius C.

I texted Josue, letting him know that I was finally en-route to his apartment. After exiting my neighborhood, I glanced towards my rear view mirror to check for oncoming cars headed towards me before I merged onto the right lane. While my eyes lingered on the road behind me, the crazy amount of survival gear and junk food behind the front seats attracted my attention and sparked a chain of contemplative thought as I assessed the gravity of my situation.

We both quit our jobs at the local pizzeria to free up a one week window to go treasure hunting. As I approached Josue's house I noticed an empty parking spot that was normally occupied by Josue's Yamaha R1 motorbike. Unfazed by that unusual sight, I parked my car in front of the sidewalk bridging the gap between the road and his apartment building's stairwell.

Josue sent me a text explaining how his bike had been towed away moments before I arrived and he was trying to figure out where to instruct his mom to leave the bike. I proceeded to call him as I grew impatient due to my excitement caused by our impending departure.

"Leave the bike at my place dumbass! We're going to be gone all week long anyways. We'll take care of it when we get back! Let's leave already!" I yelled into my phone before hanging up.

Finally, after five minutes I saw Josue make his way down the stairs carrying a rucksack on one shoulder and a tent on the other. He looked like he had been planning his entrance since January! He was decked out with brown hiking boots, sunglasses, and a bag filled with delicious junk foods and assortments of carbonated drinks. I rolled down my window as he approached the passenger seat door.

"I hate to put a stop to your pimp walk but I have to make room for that before we can leave!" I said with a sorry look on my face.

"Alright… open the trunk so we can leave!" replied Josue as he walked towards the back of my car.

I gazed over my shoulder to make sure nothing fell over and crushed him while he played Tetris with all our luggage. After he wedged the tent under all the jackets and food supplies, he opened up the back seat to drop off his bag. He set his bag down and reached into the bag to pull out two objects that I couldn't make out over my headrest.

"I got you a gift for the trip!" said Josue as he got back into the passenger side of the car.

"Oh yeah, what's that?" I replied.

"I got you a flask from Abercrombie. I know you were saying something about a bottle of Jack for the mountains."

"Right back there. Let's wait till we get out of Georgia first," I said as I motioned towards the underside of my seat.

We pulled out of his neighborhood and stopped at the nearest gas station for energy drinks and cigarettes and then we were Tennessee-bound.

Chapter 6: Tourists

I strongly believe that a fifty mile drive with anyone will extinguish any preexisting awkwardness and reservations clouding anyone's judgement. Such was the case for Josue and I as we approached the Tennessee border. Before the trip we were just friends that would hang out occasionally for a quick smoke and video game session. Three hours in we were talking about the existence of multidimensional beings and the culture shocks we both faced as bi national young adults!

There weren't any dull moments at all during the first leg of the trip as we began to accept that we were stuck with each other for the rest of the week. As a matter of fact, the running gag that we kept alive while still on the east coast was that it was 'too late to go home' anytime someone mentioned anything related to Georgia. We were so far I was surprised we had even made it that far in the first place.

The drive itself was more effective than any therapy I could ever go to! The immense pleasure I felt upon crossing the Tennessee border reminded me of what it felt like to be a little kid. Although I had been to Tennessee before, the sheer sensation of venturing through uncharted lands that I had never thought about before had me more curious than ever. By this point the GPS laying in Josue's lap read 1100 miles between us and our starting point in Santa Fe, New Mexico. I could sense the same excitement coming from Josue's side of the car, so I decided to keep him busy with a verbal survey of the drive so far.

"100 miles away from home. 1100 miles away from potentially finding treasures in the Rockies. How you holdin' up?" I asked.

"Thank you for dragging me along! I've been waiting to go on a road trip for years now. It's impossible to do stuff like that with three jobs," replied Josue as he slowly warmed up to the distance.

"Hypothetically, if we find this treasure… what are you going to do with your half?"

"Honestly, for the past three years I've been living off a thousand dollars per month. At first it sucked and I felt super poor. Now I make way more than a thousand a month, but I still only need a thousand a month. It's weird but I'm happier with my life right now even though I can afford more stuff! So I think I would just start the bar up and work there full time," answered Josue with a look of sincerity and pride on his face.

"That's stupid! You'd still have so much money left over after the bar. I'm going to invest in real estate and guitars," I replied as I hit the shuffle button on my road-trip playlist.

Rocketman, by Elton John, abruptly ended our conversation as we both couldn't resist the urge to sing along to the first verse. I looked around for my cigarettes only to find that I had left my Newport's beside Josue's Camel Crush's in the glove compartment. Before I could say anything,

Josue lit one of each brand of cigarettes and handed me mine with the brown filter fitted on it. I nodded at him in appreciation as I continued my soulful rendition of the chorus of the song. The moment couldn't have been more perfect -- that is, until the song ended and my body decided to remind me that my time to switch seats with Josue had arrived.

Chapter 7: Weather Palette

After switching seats, I realized we needed a rotation plan in order to survive the rest of the drive. Concerns regarding sleep, food, and mental health needed to be addressed before we were ready to make the switch again.

So it was decided that after every time we switched seats, the passenger seat's occupant's responsibility was to get as hammered as he could and fall asleep while the driver persevered the long roads. Much to my excitement of finally receiving the opportunity the take a break, the sheer joy of not commandeering my car made the sleep part almost non-existent.

I was alright with that at first. However, what happened during Josue's shift nearly caused us to turn back towards home.

"It's a sign! I wasn't ready for this!" exclaimed Josue as we headed towards the other end of the Tennessee border bound towards Alabama with rain pouring over our heads so hard that the road in front of us was barely visible. I felt legally blind just sitting in the passenger seat! As we approached the suspension bridge near the border, our attention was drawn towards the sound of ice hitting the roof of my car.

Might I remind you that the month of our departure was March.

I instructed Josue to slow down and began searching on my phone the cause of this strange phenomenon we were witnessing in front of us. To my surprise, it turned out that a snow storm had been making its rounds around the East coast and was forecasted to stay there for two weeks or so.

Sure enough, as I finished reading that update, the sky glistened with a white hue that resembled snowfall. Five miles later, it turned out to be snowfall indeed.

I reached to our jackets in the trunk and turned up the heater. The windows on the tiny Prius instantly began to freeze up, as did my body. There was one last thing that neither of us had thought of that could heat up the car.

I lit two cigarettes for Josue and I and began playing Christmas music on my car's speakers. All of a sudden, Vince Guaraldi's Peanut's classics and Michael Bublé's covers raised our car's temperature from cold spring to warm winter. I kept surveying the map of the snowstorm and noticed that it cleared up around the border of Alabama and Mississippi.

Once we reached the Mississippi border, the snow halted almost instantly and the rain subsided to a bare minimum. We pulled over in a tiny wood-built gas station to make a quick rest stop. As an act of some sort of victory celebration, I decided to purchase some of my favorite snacks while I waited for Josue to do his own round of shopping.

I walked to the passenger seat of the car with a bag of purple Doritos in one hand and a couple of Twix bars in the other. I lit one of my Newport's as Josue walked out with his own handful of goodies.

Of all his snacks, the first thing that I noticed on top of that pile was a bundle of Twix bars. Without saying anything I held mine up in the air while he walked towards the car and we both entered the car laughing with a sense of understanding and relief – given that we had just survived literal hell on the East coast.

"It's too late for second thoughts now, brother," I said jokingly.

"Well it's a good thing I'm not having any then," he replied.

Chapter 8: Friendly Reminder

As we reached the Oklahoma border I remembered a good friend of mine who lived there. His name was Nick Polito and he was one of the best friends I had my senior year in high school. Albeit two years younger than me, I always loved him like a little brother. Unfortunately due to his parent's financial status, he had to relocate to Oklahoma. Crossing the border made me remember the events leading up to his move. His strained relationship with his parents, his past life involved with drugs, his depression, I felt extremely guilty knowing that there was nothing else I could do to continue taking care of him after he left.

Naturally, when we entered Oklahoma my first instinct was to call Nick. Regrettably for me it was nearly midnight so we could only text. Nonetheless, he still committed to making us burgers at 2 am. During my texts with Nick a certain spell of lethargy had been cast upon me and I started to seriously consider spending the night in Oklahoma.

And if you thought I might've felt bad, imagine what Josue must've felt like after driving that entire shift.

Nick had offered us his place to crash for the night provided we reached before 4 am. He texted us an address that read two hours away from the border, so we changed our course and began to head towards Nick's house.

For the entire duration of that drive Nick kept sending us pictures of his ground beef patties and drink collections - enticing us to reach his house even sooner than previously expected. I mean, these burgers were going to be made from the freshest Kobe beef and the vegetables sautéed by a professional chef! Josue and I grew hungry exponentially picture after picture.

Finally after two hours, we approached the last right turn of the drive… which brought us to an abandoned farm in the middle of North Oklahoma. Confused, I proceeded to call Nick despite past restrictions.

"Hey check the address you sent us!" I ordered.

"Oh sh*t!" replied Nick. "I'll send you the correct one in a second. Imma hang up now."

I put in the newly arrived address into my GPS to find that his apartment was four hours away from our current location.

'Screw it' I thought to myself. You may be wondering what I was deciding to abandon. I turned to Josue who was ready to fall asleep the moment he had a chance.

"Let's just go to New Mexico in one shot. I'll take over and we'll switch whenever I feel tired," I suggested.

"Thank god. Let your friend know," replied Josue.

I texted Nick and told him how far we were and that we could stop at his place on our way back to Georgia. Naturally he was a little upset, but he agreed to host us a week later on our way back home.

Now in the driver's seat, I put on my game face and prepared to get us to New Mexico in one shot.

Chapter 9: 50/50

Now fueled with nothing else but adrenaline, cigarettes, and Peace Tea cans, I was committed to making the final stretch in one single shot. Just as I hit the fifty mile mark on the way to the Texas border I heard a shrill beeping noise coming from my gas tank indicator.

My tank was almost near empty!

I pulled up the nearest gas stations on my GPS only to find that the nearest one was 54 miles away.

Panicking, I attempted to wake up Josue from his deep slumber. Unfortunately, he continued to sleep despite my loud rants and shoulder punches. I was disappointed that the original plan proved to be ineffective as my attempts to wake up Josue bared no apparent results. The combination of my lack of sleep and my panic stricken psyche didn't help me any better.

So I resorted to trying to make it to the nearest gas station with my near empty tank. And I made it to the location… only to find that the outdated GPS had taken me to a ghost town with an abandoned gas station that hadn't been utilized in years. I stepped out of my car in frustration.

"Yo what the f*ck are you doing?" asked a drowsy Josue.

"We're f*cked bro. I'm out of gas and the nearest station is now 34 miles away from us."

"Well an empty should still get us there! Especially with a hybrid."

"An empty tank got us here!"

"F*ck that I think we can make it. I'm going back to bed."

"Alright I'll wake you up when I reach the next station… if we do reach one."

I was answered by Josue's silence in slumber. By some grace of god, I found it reassuring. So I went ahead and began driving.

My drowsiness now so ever persistent, I started to doubt my ability to drive to the next stop. Now out of energy drinks and food, my anxiety kicked in again. Nonetheless, I kept driving into the darkness.

We entered a dark stretch of road that was illuminated by bright, flashing, red lights. Unaware of the purpose of these lights I assumed that they were the landmark for an alien space base centered in Texas. The closer I got to these lights the closer I came to my conclusion as to what they were.

They turned out to be windmills.

That killed all the excitement that was keeping me awake. Fortunately, my GPS said to me that we were close. As I crept closer to the gas station I grew more awake. I was feeling more motivated every mile I drove, striving to reach my destination so that I could switch with Josue.

The road grew brighter as the lights of civilization illuminated the exit ahead of me. Without even conferring with my GPS I merged onto the exit right before the New Mexico border. The large gas station immediately drew my attention. Without a chance to think, I ran inside to grab some energy drinks and snacks. The cashier asked about my destination, hinting that she had the same conversation with many other cross country drivers. Regardless, I carried on with the conversation and went out to fill up my tank with petroleum.

After all that was settled I began to wake up Josue to switch seats as I was dead from my mini-nightmare.

Chapter 10: Coyote

Josue refused to wake up. Even though he refused to interrupt his slumber, 1100 miles into the road trip now, everything was going by the plan. I was worried Josue would begin to hate me after the first couple of hours, but against all odds, we just ended up closer than ever. After filling up gas at the Valero in Texas, I pulled onto the dark I-40 and drove speed limit until we met our first friend of the night on the empty interstate.

Expletives shot out of my mouth like bullets from a rifle.

The suicidal coyote ran into the middle of the dimly lit I-40 while I was doing a mere 75. I slammed my foot on the brakes and did one last blind spot check before I swerved into the left lane of the unoccupied road.

Just as I thought I was cleared for departure the young white coyote stopped dead in its tracks and made eye contact with me for a brief moment before running towards the bright light in multiple shipments.

I turned on my hazard lights and forced my car onto the shoulder lane near the marker for the 310 mile. All I could think about was the thankful look in the coyote's eyes moments before its passing. The funny detail that stood out the most is that the coyote ran out onto the road at 5am on a fenced road cleared of any wildlife dangers.

I turned to Josue, also turning off the car, and tried to wake him up from his six hour power nap. In darkness I heard the twitch of his foot gently rustling against the crumpled up wrappers of the Twix bars and Doritos bags.

"Yo! What was that?" he asked, unaware of the facts but only aware of the loud, harsh, hit on the passenger side of the car.

"We hit something! It looked like a white dog or something. Can I use your phone to make a call?"

"Oh sh*t! There's my phone. What're we going to do?" he asked as he grabbed his phone suspended in mid-air, hanging by its charging cable connected to my car's dashboard.

Josue swiped his thumb on the phone and handed it to me with the virtual keypad pulled up on the phone app. I grabbed the phone and proceeded to call 911.

"Hello 911 interstate emergencies. What seems to be the problem?" asked the caffeine fueled phone operator.

"We hit a coyote, our car's totaled and we're stranded in the middle of nowhere!" I replied.

"That sounds like it's on New Mexico territory. Would you mind if I put you on hold for a moment while I connect you to the nearest state trooper?" said the operator.

"Only if the hold noise is replaced by the elevator jazz music!" I joked, hoping to ease my panic with some mild, dry humor.

"Haha. I honestly, have no idea what even plays while we have you on hold. Jokes aside we found an officer 30 miles away from the state borders. Give me one second while

I patch you to him.," said the 911 operator before she greeted me with two minutes of radio silence.

"Um… Hello sir. Do you know your nearest mile marking?" asked the state trooper, distracting me from my trembling body.

"Uh, let me check, give me one second," I replied.

I flashed my car's high beam to check the road in front of me for any indication of my present location. Upon looking a half mile ahead I noticed the rays of light reflect off a long, vertical green sign.

Bingo! A mile marker!

Unfortunately, the numbers on the marker were too small for me to be legible.

"I see a marker in front of me. If you could stay on the line for a few minutes, I'm going to have to jog up there real quick," I said.

"No problem. I'll be right by the phone," assured the officer with a warm tone.

I pulled off my blue Polo windbreaker that substituted as a blanket in the 40 degrees Centigrade weather and grabbed a Newport as I left my Prius to jog to the marker.

"Unlock the doors if they lock while I'm gone," I said to Josue before he lost his battle to drowsiness.

I stepped outside to be greeted by the chilling air drag from a trucker doing a smooth 65 two feet away from me. I laced up my black Nike SB shoes and started to jog down the shoulder lane.

About 0.2 miles in I had to stop as my sleep deprived body couldn't handle the freezing weather and occasional passing truck.

"I'm halfway there. Just need a quick breather," I told the patient officer.

I shuffled through my right pocket of my black Levi jeans trying to feel for a lighter with my numbed fingertips. Upon finding the hidden lighter, I placed a Newport in between my lips and attempted to reheat my slowly freezing body.

After several tries, I finally managed to get the lighter working and all of a sudden it felt like summer.

I began jogging soon after finishing the cigarette and eventually came face to face with the glowing green sign.

"We're at the 310 mile mark!" I screamed into the phone's microphone.

"Cool just stay put, keep your hazard lights on and I'll be there as soon as possible," said the officer before ending the call.

I turned around and stared at the flashing lights on my car and took a deep, melancholic, breath before starting my jog back to the car. It was at that moment that I knew it was going to be a long week.

Chapter 11: Cops and Robbers

Still trying to process what happened over the past two hours, I began to play video games with Josue as a means of escaping my present horrors. We played the entire two hours until I decided I had had enough screen time. Josue decided to stay inside while I grabbed a Newport and went to the hood of my car.

Just as I lit my cigarette, I was blinded by the flashing lights of a truck that pulled up behind our car. Thinking it was the State trooper, I walked over to the driver seat window and waved at the barely visible driver through the frosted windows. He held up his finger to the window, signaling me to wait for a minute.

I looked towards the back of the truck to find an RV linked to the bumper. The RV was covered in dust and mud, and the link to the truck appeared to be rusted. In other words, it wasn't used very often. The driver of the truck stepped out of the car and patted me on the shoulder while my attention lingered around the RV.

"Did you guys hit that Jack Rabbit back there?" he asked, clarifying the species of the victim.

"It sure didn't look like a Jack Rabbit, ha ha! Yeah, it busted the front of my car." I replied.

"Let's take a look at your car then?" he said, walking towards the front of the

Prius without halting to wait for my approval.

As we reached the front of the car, we found a knelt-down Josue rummaging through the dangling bumper as I shined my phone's flashlight over the wreckage.

The bumper was ripped clear off the front of the car. The right headlights appeared to be out of the order. What looked like coolant was gushing out of the bottom of the car. As I followed the mini-coolant waterfall, I started to notice specs of blood droplets, which all eventually converged into a huge splatter mark under my car. That's when the smell of the dead carcass hit me.

"Yeah, she's totaled," said the truck driver. "Well, we are waiting on a tow truck," I replied sarcastically.

"You guys are more than welcome to stay in my truck while you wait. We have some free space in the RV if you want to transfer your luggage there," offered the mystery man.

Boom! There was the first red flag.

I peered around the middle-aged Caucasians hipster ponytail to notice the concerned look on Josue's face.

"That's a very generous offer, but we should be fine. I don't want to keep you busy with us in the middle of nowhere!" I replied nervously, insinuating that we weren't comfortable with the offer.

"No really, it isn't a problem. We can wait until someone gets here to help," countered the persistent stranger.

By that time, Josue had already found his way back into the lifeless car. My hand carefully rested above the groove of my Opinel No.8 in my right pocket. My silence had only seemed to trigger the truck driver's interest in our company.

"My wife and I are headed through Santa Fe. Really, it wouldn't be a big deal," continued the man.

"It's fine, man. We got makeshift blankets and stuff to keep us busy. The trooper should be here any minute," I insisted.

"That's crazy, but whatever. We can wait here until someone shows up."

The stranger brushed passed me and made his way back to his car with a frustrated look on his face. You could see the flush of red on his face lit up by every passing car's headlights. I jumped into my seat and pressed the door lock button three times before I remembered to start breathing again. Looking in my rear view mirror, I made brief eye contact with the driver and his wife through their now defrosted windows.

"Yo! They're not leaving! What do we do??" I yelled as a part of my personal panic attack.

"Where is the tow truck?" I yelled out to Josue as we both bonded over the general panic covered situation we were stuck in.

We both pulled out our phones and attempted to distract ourselves from our present realities and, just when we managed to calm down, we were interrupted by a loud tapping noise from my window.

I stepped out of the car to see what the truck driver wanted, this time with my knife hidden under my jacket sleeve.

"It's freezing out here, man! Let us just drive you there. The tow truck can bring your car wherever you want to go. You don't want to be stranded here on the other side of the country in the middle of nowhere," said the truck driver with his ever-present persistency.

I took a moment to process what just came out of the man's mouth.

I never said we were from Georgia! I thought to myself. A voice in the back of my head kept insisting that I should go and warm up my iceberg body in the heated truck. Another voice said that I should stay in my car because we were going to get robbed in the middle of nowhere if I didn't. After conferring with the consciences in my head, I made my decision.

"Don't worry about us," I said.

I made my way around the truck driver and locked myself in my car. I looked at Josue, hoping to find a reassuring look on his face and, sure enough, he delivered. The man outside my window began banging on said window, yelling about how I was being stupid and other such demeaning adjectives. After ignoring him for a few minutes he gave up decided to wait in his car.

Fifteen minutes later, we saw the flashing blue and red lights approaching the service car U-turn.

The arrival of the trooper caused the truck to flee the scene, marking the end of our little nightmare. I turned off my hazard lights and ran towards the New Mexico State Trooper van. The door swung open and out came the lone officer, wide awake, carrying on his face a warm and welcoming smile. The Cherokee man introduced himself to Josue and I and began surveying the remains of our wrecked car and our poor friend of the wild, who we aptly named Wile E. Coyote.

"The tow truck on its way?" I inquired. "Will the car drive?" retorted the officer.

"If it did, we would have probably met you in Santa Fe," I joked.

"Well, the tow truck is going to be another hour or so. You guys are more than welcome to seek refuge in my car. It's freezing out here for some reason. First case of the day and I'm already in my jacket!" vented the officer (full disclaimer, I can't, for the life of me, remember his name).

"Is it usually this cold in the mornings?" I asked the officer as I lit a Newport. I threw my lighter in Josue's direction, who was making his way to the barely visible ranch running parallel to the highway, for what, I imagined, a bathroom break.

"Not usually. You could say I'm a bit unfortunate to have to deal with it, but that doesn't really mean much in light of your situation, I suppose," joked the officer as he unlocked the back-door of his van.

"Time to get comfortable in the back of a cop car," I said jokingly to Josue after he returned.

The officer advised me to contact my insurance provider while he was filling out his case report.

After Josue sat in the car, I told him to let my folks back home in Georgia know what happened.

Chapter 12: Damage Control

Soon after I got into the car, I received a call back from my insurance company and simultaneously was handed an incident report to fill out. Being six feet tall in the back of a cop car with a phone in one hand and a pen in the other was not by any means easy, so I had to step back out into the cold, barely lit streets.

I stood in front of the car door and used the window as a support for the flimsy sheet of paper fluttering with the wind. Josue, in the meantime, began patiently explaining how we were going to be stuck in New Mexico for a week to our family, friends, and significant others. The sun slowly began to rise as I filled out the incident report.

It illuminated a beautiful desert landscape with the Rockies barely visible dozens of miles away from us. The emergency lane had a fence running parallel to the road on both sides of it, stretching out for miles.

My insurance company managed to get ahold of a tow truck willing to drive us more than 100 miles to the nearest city; I decided to get comfortable in the cop car as we waited for it.

The tow truck arrived after an hour and a half and the cop left soon after. The remains of the car were visible under the morning sun as the tow truck driver stepped out of his truck and began moving around the dented car parts. He hooked the Prius up to the tow truck and Josue began throwing the wreckage onto the truck. For some reason the tow truck driver was not open to Josue's help.

"Yo, leave that s*it there!" exclaimed the tow truck driver.

"Sorry bro. You need to chill the f*ck out," said Josue with a calming tone. Unfortunately, that's not how the truck driver heard it.

"No, you need to chill f*ck out!" yelled the tow truck driver.

"Man screw this, you can get shotgun!" retorted Josue in my direction.

After the car was stowed on the back of the tow truck, I made my way to the front seat of the truck, and that's when my lethargy hit me - I hadn't slept since we left Georgia.

Shortly after the drive started, I was fast asleep; it was time to get used to sleeping any chance I could get.

Chapter 13: Santa Rosa, NM (Not Cali)

By the time I woke up, my Prius was back on the ground. Stepping out of the car, I saw the highway exit to my left and a two mile road to my right. The tow truck lot was populated with mainly out-of-state cars. I hopped out of the truck and noticed the blood and fur stains all over the front of my car; soon after, I decided to brave the dead animal stench and grab a Newport from the front seat. Josue soon followed for his Camel Crushes after he climbed out of the truck. After grabbing the cigarettes, I locked the car with all our essentials still in it.

Santa Rosa was essentially a 2 mile stretch of road with gas stations, rest stops, and a tow truck company. There was sand everywhere and you couldn't even see the mountains from the city. After leaving the tow truck lot, I received a call from my insurance agency telling me that they managed to secure me a rental car... 150 miles from our current location and that another tow truck was on its way to take the Prius to a body shop. Starving, Josue and I began walking down the long stretch of road in search of food.

According to our phones, the temperature outside was 86 degrees Fahrenheit and, naturally, we were dying in the scorching sun with our black clothes. The nearest gas station was a mile away from the tow truck lot and somehow we took half an hour to get there.

The gas station was huge. There were movie screening rooms, showers, multiple bathrooms, a Subway, and plenty more! Totally ignoring our stomachs, we began perusing the countless aisles for any souvenirs we could find and finally ended up purchasing 2 Maruchan ramen bowls. When we finished microwaving our food, I called my insurance company for an ETA on the tow truck.

"So when's the tow truck going to get here?" I asked.

"It should be there right now. Are you not there?" replied the agent. I spit out my food as soon as I heard that.

"I gotta run!" I said as I hung up.

Josue and I left our food at the tables to get to the tow truck as soon as we could. After all, all our money, food, chargers, and other essentials were in the car.

We ran the mile back as fast as we could until we saw a huge tow truck pass us.

"I see the car!" yelled Josue.

Chapter 14: Hitchhikers Guide to the Middle of Nowhere

We stood on the sidewalk of the single road in the city as we watched to tow truck drive right past us with my car on it. I still had the keys, both of our phones were dying, all of our survivor gear was in the car, and most of our money was in the back seat.

Obviously, we were screwed.

Naturally, the first step was to figure out where the car was being sent to. After making a couple of phone calls, I got an address that was about thirty miles away from our current location - a body shop in the middle of nowhere. The next step was to figure out where the rental car was so that we could get to the Prius. After another couple of phone calls, we found out that the rental car was all the way in Santa Fe, New Mexico.

With no where else to go, Josue and I made our way back to the tow truck shop and tried to plan out our next move. While there, a man named Mike offered to drive us to the rental car for $150, but Josue promptly refused the offer and suggested we attempt hitchhiking to the rental car.

I agreed, so we headed towards the interstate with our thumbs extended as far as they could.

And we walked.

Walked in the scorching New Mexico sun for hours. By the end of our little hitchhiking spell we barely made it a mile or two down the road.

"Dude, we have no choice! We have to take up Mike on his offer!" I yelled, frustrated, at Josue.

"Nah bro! That's so much money!" responded Josue.

"Well, what the f*ck are we supposed to do then, huh? We have no more money left, no way to get to the Prius and our phones are on the verge of dying!" I retorted.

Josue eventually gave up and we headed to the nearest ATM machine in Santa Rosa and began withdrawing the last of our money. We approached Mike at the tow truck shop soon after, attempting to negotiate terms one last time.

"Can you do $100?" asked Josue.

"Ok, just pay for my gas too," responded Mike.

Josue, feeling proud, hopped into Mike's beat up van and motioned me to sit in the front seat.

Upon reaching the gas station, Mike filled up about forty dollars' worth of gas in his car, making him a fair profit as we had to pay for gas both ways of the trip.

And, just like that, we were off to Santa Fe.

Chapter 15: Going down to New Mexico

… or so we thought.

Mike had to pick his son up from school so we were forced to tag along on the detour. He missed the turn to his son's school by five blocks and ended up driving in reverse for the entirety of the missed distance. Finally, we reached his son's school and soon after, we found out that his son had thrown one of his shoes onto the roof of the school. This kid was about six years old and we were impressed he even got the shoe up that high.

Anyway, that added quite some time to the drive as we had to wait for a janitor to bring the shoe down.

"Are we dropping him home?" I asked.

"No, he's coming along," Mike replied.

We set out onto the interstate entrance Josue and I had previously attempted hitchhiking. And the drive was beautiful.

The scenery included the Rockies on one side and plain desert on the other. It was just us and the road. No traffic, no bystanders, just plain desert roads. Halfway through the trip, Mike offered to sell us some weed and that was that.

Chapter 16: Santa Fe

After driving for an hour and a half, we finally reached something that bore some resemblance to a city. We had made it to Santa Fe. Mike drove us to the car shop, asked for the forty dollar gas refill, and left us at the car rental shop.

Josue and I walked into the car rental shop and waited in line for a couple of minutes until it was our turn.

"My insurance said they booked us a car. Is it ready?" I asked the Enterprise employee.

The employee glanced at his screen, clicking away for a few moments, and replied, "It doesn't look like we have anything for you at the moment sir. I'm really sorry about that."

"God d*mnit!" exclaimed Josue.

I proceeded to call my insurance company in the middle of the store.

"They don't have a car for me! What the f*ck am I supposed to do? Your tow truck towed my car away without us even knowing about it and now we're stranded in the middle of f*cking nowhere with no way of getting around!" I calmly spoke into my phone (Just kidding, everyone heard every word of what I said).

"Hey kid, come over here for a second," said the Enterprise employee.

I walked over to the service counter and hung up on my insurance company.

"We do actually have one car left. I'm sorry to hear about your story so we are going to give you guys the last car," replied the employee sympathetically.

"Bitching!" I replied. First win of the day.

We followed the employee outside to the parking lot. Outside, there were a couple of trucks and other various sedans parked on the lot. But out of all the cars, one car stood out the most. It was a beautiful silver-colored Dodge Dart.

And for some reason, the employee kept walking towards it. When he hit the unlock button on his car keys and the Dodge flashed, everything hit Josue and I all at once.

We were about to drive the Dodge Dart for the next couple of days!

We hopped in the car and set course for the Prius back in Santa Rosa.

Chapter 17: Syncing Up

The drive back to Santa Rosa took only an hour, thanks to the horsepower of the Dart. After reaching the two mile strip, we began a 30 mile drive that consisted of driving past a correctional facility, cows in the middle of dirt roads and roads that weren't even on our GPS. Lost for a little while, we kept ending back up at the prison, until we finally made it to the body shop.

The body shop was at a dead end of one of the dirt roads and all it consisted of was a little house with an extended garage. The beat up Prius was sitting outside the house, covered in sand and animal extracts. We parked the Dart and knocked on the house door; out walked a man with a beer in his hand.

"Hey there, my name's Anthony. You must be Mihir," said Anthony.

"Hey man, thanks so much for all your help. Do you know how long it'll be until the car is ready?" I asked.

"The parts will be at least a week until they arrive. But I'll call you when it's ready. Any of you guys want a drink?"

"Hell yeah! Also, can we quickly transfer all our luggage to the rental?" I asked.

"No worries, go for it. Let me go grab a Bud," said Anthony as he walked back inside.

Josue and I began with the trunk luggage: our clothes, the tent, sleeping bags and all our food. After the trunk, we unloaded the entire luggage in the seats into the Dodge Dart. Anthony soon returned with one beer.

"Ok bro, you're driving," I said to Josue.

"And you guys are 21," joked Anthony as he winked at me.

I finished the drink and we hopped in the Dart, ready to finally begin our treasure hunt - except it was nearly midnight and so we had to spend the night at our starting point. We put in the address to Ojo Caliente in Santa Fe and began driving.

We barely made it by two in the morning after driving a couple of hours. We approached the security guard of the RV lot.

"It's a little too late to make reservations but if you guys stay in your car, just remember to book a spot tomorrow morning," said the security guard. Win number two of the day.

We drove around the dark RV lot until we found a vacant spot and left the heaters on for an hour to warm up the car before trying to catch some shut-eye before the sun came up.

It was finally time to start treasure hunting.

Chapter 18: Round 1

The sun barely shone at seven in the morning, and so did Josue and I. Nevertheless, the drive for finding treasure kept us up.

The treasure map was included in one of Mr. Forrest Fenn's memoirs and along with that, in another memoir, was a cryptic poem that was said to reveal 9 clues about the whereabouts of the treasure's location. After we hit the road, we began deciphering the poem and looking at the map. Unfortunately, we found it hard to eat on an empty stomach, so we decided to stop at a gas station to grab some munchies.

I went in and bought my usual Doritos chile lime flavor with a couple of Twix bars and Josue bought himself a bag of Cheetos, Munchies, and another couple of Twix bars. After we finished in the gas station mart, we stored all of our opened bags in the glove compartment of the passenger seat. Up top on the roof of the car, there was a sunglass compartment.

That's going to be filled with food by the time this trip ends, I thought to myself. We continued driving in the still, dusky darkness of the morning until we happened upon a little town called La Madera. It was at this point that we decided to wait for the sun to rise completely. In the meantime, we decided to dedicate the hour to further deciphering the poem.

One of the clues mentioned the phrase *in the wood*. To our surprise, the city we were in, literally translated to *the wood*. So we figured we were on the right path.

After the sun rose, the little town became more visible. There were little cottages bustled together on one streets and on the other end of that streets was a little post office that looked closed. Apart from that, the rest of the town consisted of fields and a river that ran parallel to the road we were on. Based on our analysis of the poem, we decided to drive alongside the river.

It began at ground level and then lead us up some of the tallest peaks of the Rocky mountains. We sat comfortably about 8,000 feet above sea level at one point when we stepped out of the car to brush our teeth and look for the treasure. At this little stopping point, we found the remains of a burned down house, which we interpreted as a clue. Going through the remains, Josue found a signed baseball and a couple other little trinkets that I can't remember off the top of my head. After deciding the treasure wasn't anywhere near us, we began climbing up the 12,000-foot high mountain by foot just for fun. We trekked up the mountainside for an hour until we reached the top and looked down on the snow-covered mountain tops and desert-filled floor of the New Mexico ground.

After trudging back down, we continued driving up the mountain until we met our first friend of the day. As we approached a downhill slope on a straight road, we saw someone walking their dog at the bottom of the hill and we rolled down to him and rolled down our windows.

"Hey man, do you need a ride somewhere?" we asked the stranger.

"No thank you, I'm good. But if you guys have any alcohol that would be awesome!" replied the stranger.

"We can give you a shot! We have some Jack Daniels in the backseat," replied Josue. I reached into the backseat to grab one of our flasks and handed it to the stranger.

"So where are you headed?" I asked the stranger.

"I'm walking to work right now. It's only a ten mile walk. I like bringing my dog with me for company," replied the stranger.

Josue looked at the GPS and it showed that we were on an unknown road and that we were very close to the Colorado border. The river kept flowing towards the Colorado border so we asked the stranger for directions.

"Hey man, do you know how to get to Colorado from here?" I asked.

Now I don't remember the exact directions but it did involve navigating through multiple dirt roads. We even passed a boy scout excursion group and asked them for directions. But ultimately the roads started sloping downhill and we knew we were on the right track. Eventually, our tires met with the desert sand once again and we turned left onto the interstate and followed the signs to Denver, Colorado.

Chapter 19: Denver, CO

Finally after a couple dozen miles, we reached the border of Colorado - the land of dispensaries. There were at least three dispensaries in the border town alone. We were in awe at the number of people just lighting up in the middle of the streets. Most notably, there was a Wake and Bake hotel located near an abandoned train track running alongside the highway. Unfortunately for the two of us, neither of us was 21 at the time so we were unable to see what the big fuss was concerning home-grown marijuana. We continued driving until we reached downtown Denver.

Downtown Denver was polluted with monotone skyscrapers and traffic. Nonetheless, it was captivating enough that Josue and I decided to spend the rest of the day exploring the city. We parked the Dart in a parking garage in the heart of the downtown and began walking around by foot. We ended up at a bus station where we saw a group of people smoking pot. A woman and man approached us and asked us if we wanted to partake, and we said yes.

"My name's Lilith by the way. And this is James. I just met him today!" said the woman as she pointed to her friend.

From this point, on every two blocks we walked we were smoked out by someone. It was incredible. After the fifth session, Josue and I decided to walk around the city on our own and go sightseeing. Coincidentally it was also St. Patrick's Day, but we were unaware so we kept guessing at why everyone around us was dressed in green.

We found a beautiful little Ethiopian shop with falafels, gyros, and shawarma so we decided to stop for some dinner. It was at this time Josue revealed that he had never tried a gyro before.

"It's on me this time. You need to try this. I'm going to get us two chicken shawarmas," I said.

"I don't know if I'm going to finish it bro. It smells weird in here," replied Josue.

Regardless of his pessimism, I ordered away. After five minutes, our food was ready, wrapped in aluminum foil, and in our hands. I dove right into my wrap while Josue struggled with the foil. Eventually, he managed to uncover his middle-Eastern burrito and took a bite.

"Holy s*it! This is so good! Why have you never shown me this before?" exclaimed Josue.

"I told you it was good," I replied, smirking.

We took the wraps to go and continued walking around until we reached the city's convention center. This building consisted of glass windows stacked on top of each other for a couple hundred feet into the air. But what really caught our eyes was the companion sculpture of a big bear pounding on the glass. Two blocks away we ran into Lilith and James again.

We found them after James snuck up behind Josue and scared the life out of him by yelling super loud. We said our goodbyes and they left us with some wax concentrates

from a homeless man to smoke for the rest of
the trip (Don't worry, I've already been on
trial for it).

We set out to find the parking garage
after spending eight hours in Denver. Eight
hours. We were ready to head back to our
make shift home in New Mexico and found the
parking garage and hopped back into the
Dart, starting to drive back to Ojo
Caliente.

Chapter 20: Slowing Down

It was pretty late in the night and there was not another car in sight. Struggling with slumber again, I decided to call it quits after we crossed the New Mexican border. We found a little motel and rented out a room for the night.

After taking turns showering, we decided to get drunk off our asses and go to bed to get an early start the next day. Josue was elated about the idea of getting a good night's sleep on a real bed rather than sleeping in the car, and we played Mario Party for a couple of hours before Josue called it a night.

Unfortunately for me, I had a severe case of the insomnias. By this point in the story, I felt like we had a pretty cool story to tell, so I walked over to a nearby gas station and purchased a green notebook and a Uniball ink pen… and some ramen. Once I got back to the motel room, I rolled myself a dirty cigarette, a cigarette with wax concentrates (I came up with that term), and began writing this book that you are reading right now. I even emailed one of my composition professors to let her know that I was writing a new book. After finishing the first chapter by hand, I decided to call it a night myself and went to bed.

We woke up the next morning at around seven thirty and ate two ramens before heading back to La Madera and resuming our treasure hunt. Josue offered to drive after he read all the writing I had done the night before.

"You got something special there, bro. Keep writing in the car," he said before getting into the Dart.

"F*ck that, I'm going back to bed," I said before passing out in the back seat.

I slept for the entirety of the ride but still managed to get a peek at the beautiful sunrise before falling asleep.

Chapter 21: Round 2

We finally made it back to La Madera an hour and a half later to resume the hunt. This time, we went back to the proverbial drawing board and decided following the river again, as it was our best bet at finding the treasure. We believed the river was supposed to lead to a waterfall; all that was remaining was to find the waterfall.

And so we followed the river. After driving for twenty minutes, we reached a downhill road that was familiar to us. And the reason it was so familiar was because at the end of the road we spotted our friend from last time. We pulled up beside him.

"You have to let us give you a ride this time!" I said.

"Alright, alright. I'm headed home. It's just down this road," he said as he hopped in the now empty backseat.

"What's your name, bro?" asked Josue.

"Louie, like the comedian. So what are you boys doing out here in New Mexico?" replied the stranger on the road… well, not much of a stranger anymore.

"We're just sightseeing. Currently looking for a waterfall," I responded.

"There's a waterfall five minutes away from my house! I can show you there. Just give me a few minutes to drop some things off at home," Louie responded.

We kept driving down the straight road until it split off to two separate cities.

We ended up taking the left turn to Petaca, Louie's home town.

Upon reaching the little town, the first thing we noticed was that it was so small, you could count all the houses just from the entrance. The only semblance of a store was an illegal bootleg alcohol store and a little shack in front of a farm.

"I'm going to get some of my friends real quick," said Louie while stepping out of the car without giving us a chance to respond; he sounded excited to show us around so we went with it.

After waiting for five minutes, he came back with a couple that looked like they were in their forties. Keep in mind the car was filled with all sorts of sh*t and there was barely enough legroom for one passenger in the back seat. Somehow, all three of the Petaca residents managed to fit into the back of the Dart. Once the doors closed, we noticed that everyone reeked of booze.

Regardless, we continued following their directions up the stream until they told us to turn left onto what seemed like the forest. There were barely visible tracks covered with huge stones in the path and they wanted us to turn onto it. Josue nervously guided the car through the pathway until we heard a loud screeching noise underneath the car. We decided to not take any further chances and made our way to the waterfall on feet.

After navigating through the forest for ten minutes, we eventually made it to the waterfall, and boy was it beautiful. The water fell from at least a hundred feet off

a cliff onto the river we were following.
There was even a mini water tunnel that the
locals used to used as a slide in their
youth. Louie pulled out a bottle of vodka
and I decided to spend some time drinking
with Louie and talking about the small town
that they came from.

After spending an hour or so there we
finally got back to dropping off the couple
and resuming our search. Right after we
reached the town, Louie asked if we could
drop him off at his son's house. We agreed
and drove him to another nearby town to his
son's home. We thanked him for showing us
the falls and then set out to try and make
the most out of the remaining day light.

The rest of the trip we kept stopping
at different viewpoints to search for the
treasure, all the while listening to a
scraping sound coming from the underside of
the car.

After the sun set, we drove back to Ojo
Caliente to rent out a tent ground.

Chapter 22: Bonfire

After reaching Ojo Caliente, we paid our dues at the front desk and asked them about the spas they had.

"If you purchase a tent ground, you still have to pay thirty each for access to the spas and saunas," said the receptionist.

"We only have thirty dollars left between the two of us, can you please let us in? It's only for one night," I begged.

"Just this one time. Enjoy your stay at Ojo Caliente," responded the generous receptionist.

We got our passes and headed to the campgrounds. After parking our car, we pulled the tent out of the trunk and began setting it up. I took charge of the tent while Josue focused his attention on the car to assess the damage done by the stray rock.

"So a piece of plastic is sticking out of the car but I can MacGyver the sh*t out of it though," said Josue while pulling out his gym sack from the back seat.

"Thank god! Let's get some tools then," I replied as Josue pulled out a plier and hammer out of his bag.

"Never mind, you do your thing," I said as I resumed my work with the tent.

Josue finished working on the car by the time I was done with the tent. The weather outside was quite pleasant too, so we decided to make our way to the hot springs, spas, and saunas that the receptionist mentioned.

Josue and I grabbed our bathing suits from the car and entered the resort's locker rooms. I got out first and made my way to the nearest hot spring, while Josue soon followed and took a seat under a mini waterfall beside me.

"F*ck dude this is so relaxing!" said Josue.

"Yeah dude this f*cking rocks!" I replied.

"Excuse me, could you stop saying that please," said a random man next to Josue.

"Stop saying what? F*ck?" responded Josue while I couldn't contain my laughter.

"Yes, that word. We're trying to relax here," said the lonely man. By this point everyone was looking at him with disgust on their faces.

"Alright, alright, we'll leave," I said, barely catching my breath.

We went to the next nearest hot spring and kept circling the rest of the amenities for the next two hours until we decided to go back to the tent.

While in the locker room, Josue asked me if we could cook our dinner on a bonfire as, after he revealed, he had never started a fire before.

"I guarantee we'll have a bonfire tonight," I assured.

Just as we exited the spa resort, we noticed a communal bonfire where families were handing out smores and sharing drinks.

"Well, I guess this works too," I said as we walked towards the warmth of the bonfire like moths to a flame.

At the fire, after all the families with children left, there were three people: a married couple on vacation and a single woman named Marienne. The married couple had a daughter who took a year off from school to go travelling with her boyfriend and who also had a blog that followed her adventures. But here's where things get interesting. Marienne was recently widowed and she was a publisher for Legend magazine. You might be wondering, *what was she doing in New Mexico if not vacationing?*

Well she, just like Josue and I, was treasure hunting. The cult following that Mr. Fenn had was so established that we met a fellow treasure hunter at a random bonfire in Santa Fe! Josue and I were telling her all about where we had been, obviously without revealing too much, and she too vaguely described the adventures she had been on so far. In addition to talking about the treasure, we got to get to know each other better. She had driven all the way down to New Mexico from Mississippi. As the night grew colder with the diminishing flames of the bonfire, Josue and I began walking back to the tent grounds.

I had myself a black sleeping bag while Josue had an insulated blanket bed that I brought for him. His bed was cushioned while mine took the shape of the rocks underneath the tent. Nonetheless, I happily gave Josue the comfier bed as he had driven all day long. We spent the rest of the night drinking Jack Daniels and playing Mario party until Josue finally passed out. I pulled out a book light that I had in my bag and continued writing my book.

After writing for about an hour I decided to clock out. Unfortunately for me, I found it extremely difficult to fall asleep on the rocky floor of my sleeping bag and simultaneously deal with the cold breezes of the night, so I made my way back to the Dodge Dart, left the heater on for an hour and passed out in the car.

Chapter 23: Knockout

The next morning, I awoke to the sound of Josue tapping on the window of the driver's seat. I quickly rose, put my seat in an upright position and unlocked the car. Josue, cold from the night before, sat in the car and held his hands close to the A/C vents. I stepped outside to brush my teeth and eventually began packing up the tent. Once we were all done cleaning up the tent ground, we set out to find the treasure once again.

Without revealing too much, the drawing board discussion began a little differently. I decided to flip the poem upside down and work backwards instead of forward. After analyzing the new poem, we drove to La Madera to begin our hunt.

We followed the river again, but this time from a different angle until we hit the Petaca sign. Instead of turning left towards the falls we turned right. After driving a few miles, we reached still water and decided to park at an up hill road that lead to a flat farm ground. There were trees and bushes everywhere. This place looked like heaven. Confident in our analysis, we began surveying the surroundings. After walking a couple yards, we found a brown, broken house, in the middle of the flat grounds.

Close to this house was a dried up creek. Everything slowly started matching up with the new poem. We followed this creek until we reached a small hole dug into the ground covered by a metal sheet. After struggling to move the sheet for ten minutes we finally uncovered the hole, only to find that it was empty. We kept walking along the creek until we spotted a blaze. If you don't know what that means, that's ok. We didn't know what it was either. But we assumed it was a bunch of burnt leaves or a visibly orange or reddish object near the treasure. I can't describe what we saw but we both had the feeling we found a blaze. The blaze lead us to a tree with a dugout hole in front of it, covered by rocks and sticks.

Josue and I took turns throwing out the stones and sticks until the bottom of the hole became visible. It seemed like the perfect place to bury a treasure and all the clues seemed to add up to the location. After all the stones and sticks were removed, we were left with an empty grave site. Nothing inside of the hole. Just an empty pit. After spending all afternoon leading up to this point, both our morale's were pretty low. Pretty disappointed by the outcome, Josue and I started to make our way back to the car.

As we walked down the slope towards the car, we heard a pack of wolves howling in the distance and, petrified, we began running towards the car. The sound of footprints slowly got louder and louder as I reached into my pocket and pulled out the car keys, getting ready to make a quick escape. The wolves were coming up the road from the left and our car was on the right of the road. We barely made it into the car as we saw the pack of wolves on the other side of the road run right past us.

"This whole trip's been really fun but I think the hunt's coming to an end," I said.

"I agree. It sucks but I don't think we can find the treasure anymore. Let's just chill until the Prius is ready," said Josue.

"That's cool and all but we can't afford to pay for the tent ground every day for the rest of the trip," I replied.

"Well do you know anywhere we can stay for the next two days?" asked Josue.

"I think I have an idea," I said.

Chapter 24: Dear Dallas

I dialed an old friend's number on my phone.

"Hey Karthik, whatchu up to, brother?" I said.

"Where are you guys?" said Karthik.

"Are you in town?" I asked

"I will be in ten hours," replied Karthik.

"Bet, we'll pick you up at the airport! Can we crash at your dorm for a couple days?" I asked.

"Sure but what are you doing in Texas?" Karthik asked again.

"We're not in Texas yet, but we will be soon," I replied.

"Copy that. You can stay with me," said Karthik as he hung up.

Josue turned to me with a look of concern on his face.

"And how long does it take to get to Texas?" asked Josue.

"Don't worry about it," I said to Josue as I put in the address to the Dallas airport on my GPS. The ETA popped up on the screen.

"Eight f*cking hours! Are we going to make it in time?" asked Josue.

"With the Dart… hell yeah we're going to make it on time," I replied.

Josue drove the first four hours of the ride. This time, he saw all the things he missed on the way to New Mexico. The state entrance and exit signs. The flashing red lights as it got darker the more back in time we drove. After inching a couple miles past the flashing red lights we stopped for gas and switched seats. As I began driving, a car sped right past us at an incredibly high speed. We tailed this car for the next couple dozen miles until Josue received an Amber alert on his phone.

The alert told us that someone in a red car was driving with someone they had kidnapped. They described the car's make, model, and included the license plate's numbers. Coincidentally, the car that we were tailing also matched the aforementioned description. Since we were too far away from the car, we decided to speed up a little to check the plates.

As we inched closer and closer to the car the plates became more visible. And sure enough, it was the same car as mentioned in the Amber alert. We called the cops and notified them of our location and received praise from the Texas state trooper on the phone. Feeling heroic, we stopped to feast like kings.

Well, for some more ramen, but the feeling still lingered. After we left the gas station, we realized we had forgotten to consider the time difference. As well as this, Karthik's parents sent me the flight details, revealing that the flight had been postponed by a couple of hours. With a couple hours left to kill, despite losing an hour, I began navigating to the house my parents owned when I was still a child in my hometown of Plano.

Josue took the driver's seat once again after our ramen was finished. I decided to catch some shut eye, preparing myself for a day out in Texas.

Josue woke me up after we reached my house. I walked around the house for a couple of minutes, reminiscing about my childhood, before heading back into the car.

"So what's next?" asked Josue.

"Let's get some food!" I exclaimed.

"Where at?" asked Josue.

"I know just the spot. I'll drive us there," I replied.

I took Josue to one of my favorite Chinese restaurants in Plano before we set out for downtown Dallas.

We drove around downtown Dallas and saw all the corporate skyscrapers and the Dallas Mavericks' stadium. After walking around looking for more food, we walked back to the car and began driving towards the airport.

We reached the airport just in time to receive Karthik. He made his way out of the terminal and approached our car.

"Damn dude, what did you do to this sexy car, man!" shouted Karthik.

"You think this is bad! You should've seen the Prius! By the way I'm Josue," Josue replied.

Karthik sat in the front seat while Josue laid down in the back seat.

"Damn, I'm hungry again," I said as we began driving to a family friend's house for dinner. Josue reached for the sunglass compartment and opened it to reveal a bunch of Twix bars stacked on top of each other.

"I'm impressed," I said.

See, I told you it would have food in it eventually.

Chapter 25: Nostalgia

In this chapter I'm going to just share a couple short stories because most of the trip was dedicated to playing Mario Party, Smash Bros, and sleeping. One relevant plot point is that Anthony from the car shop informed us that the car was going to take an extra couple of days and that he would call when the car was ready.

--

On the UTD campus, I tried figuring out who else we could meet while we were stuck in Texas. To my surprise, I found out that an old friend from India was currently enrolled at UTD. I called her asking if she was doing anything and she replied, telling us that there was a Holi party going on that night and that we should come. After begging Josue to come for a couple hours, he gave up and tagged along.

As the night began, we walked past the tennis court to the Holi party. Now for those of you reading this right now with not a clue as to what Holi is, it's an Indian that worships the goddess Kali and to celebrate it, people get together and throw paint and colored powder at each other.

Josue and I wore clothes we didn't care about and walked right into the mosh pit of the American Holi rave. We spent hours throwing paint at everybody with my friend from India, Zeba and once we were done painting the crowds, we called Kathik to see where he was. He told us that he was at the tennis courts right beside the rave so I filled my hands with orange paint and ran to the tennis court.

Karthik had just about finished his game before I ran towards him, smearing the bright paint all over his face.

--

Lastly, I wanted to meet Ms. Tangela, a teacher from my childhood, before we left Texas. So we organized a lunch together.

I met her and her husband at a Thai restaurant twenty minutes away from Karthik's dorm. She was telling me all about her kids and my childhood friends and how she was writing a book, as we hadn't met in years. I proceeded to tell her about my own book and how it was slowly becoming the treasure we were looking for.

"Mihir, I think you are an incredibly smart child. You have been from the start. Be careful out there. I hope you don't get into any trouble," said Ms. Tangela.

"Don't worry about me, I'll be fine," I assured her.

Chapter 26: Farewell

Anthony called, informing us that the Prius was up and running again. We let him know we'd be there in eight hours or so. I wrote Karthik, who was in class, a letter and along with it left some gifts for him. Josue and I packed up and hit the road again to get to the car shop.

Eight hours later, we reached the car shop. Josue sat in the Prius and soon after, we left for the Enterprise in Santa Fe with Josue driving behind me.

Five exits away from Santa Fe we approached a snow storm so we had to slow down the pace a bit. After two hours, we managed to make it to the shop. Before we returned it, we transferred the entire luggage to the Prius and got the car cleaned inside and out.

We drove to Louie's house and left him a thank you letter beside a water bottle filled with Jack Daniels at his door step. On the way back we stopped at Santa Rosa to say goodbye to Mikey too. And we were off.

I drove the first shift while Josue kept me up by retelling some of the highlights of the trip. From the coyote to Texas. Everything we did in those two weeks was fondly talked about on the way back home. We barely even considered just how really f*cked the entire trip was. Although we didn't find the treasure, we ended up closer than ever. I think that's something that Forrest Fenn would have wanted.

We reached the Texas borders and noticed the flashing red lights on the windmills again and recognized all the gas stations we had crossed. Realizing how late it was, we unanimously decided to spend the night with my aunt in Arkansas.

I called my aunt to let her know we were in Texas and that we should be reaching by the afternoon of the next day. We stopped to fill up gas and switched seats. I comfortably fell asleep in the backseat knowing that this would be the last time I sleep in the car on the trip.

Chapter 27: All Falls Down

I woke up to find Josue asleep in the driver's seat. I looked outside my window to see that we were in an empty parking lot of a random hotel in Oklahoma. The time was about six thirty in the morning. I woke up Josue and told him to switch seats with me so that he could continue sleeping.

A couple hours into Oklahoma, I stopped for gas in a small rural town. After filling up gas, I walked inside the gas station's store to go to the bathroom; unfortunately, all the urinals were full so I went to the closed bathroom to relieve myself. The insides of the bathroom were littered with hate speech and conservative propaganda. The back of the bathroom door was covered in insults and racial slurs. *Apparently conservatives think of immigrants when they take a sh*t,* I thought to myself.

After I walked out of the store, I called my aunt to update her of our location. Josue and I switched seats one last time before reaching Arkansas.

We got back onto the interstate and headed towards the Arkansas exit. As we got closer and closer, we noticed more and more state troopers parked alongside the highway. We finally reached the one mile mark of the state when we noticed two state troopers parked in the middle of the two directional highway. Soon after passing them they circled around and began tailgating us. Josue thought they were trying to pass so we merged onto the right lane of the highway. They did not pass. The GPS told us to take the left exit so we merged back in front of them. And right after we saw both their lights flash.

They forced us onto the shoulder lane of the exit ramp and told Josue to step out of the car.

"We're pulling you over for an illegal lane change. Please follow me to my car," said the trooper, before leading Josue to one of the cop cars. In the meantime, I called my aunt to inform her that we had been pulled over for a traffic violation and that we may a little late. Josue returned five minutes later and sat back in the driver's seat.

"Ok so he gave me a warning for an illegal lane change. Which is bullsh*t but apparently I didn't leave enough space before merging," said Josue.

"Damn that sucks. At least it's only just a warning," I replied before getting interrupted by a tapping sound on my window. I rolled down my window to talk to the state trooper.

"Do you have any illegal immigrants, meth, or anything else illegal in the car?" asked the state trooper.

We had a little bit of weed, wax concentrates, and half a shot of Jack Daniels in the car. Harmless right?

"No sir not at all! Do we look like the kind of kids that are harboring fugitives?" I joked.

"Well then you don't have a problem if I search the car then right?" responded the unamused officer.

"I do mind. We're trying to get to Arkansas in the next hour. We're good kids, I swear. We've just had the longest two weeks and we're just trying to get home," I said with a nervous tone in my voice.

"Would you please step out of the car. Both of you. I've called in backup. We won't search your car till the K-9 gets here," replied the officer as he opened my door.

Josue and I sat on the grass beside the shoulder lane and tried to make conversation with the officer. We also left our cigarettes in the car and both of our phones were running low on battery.

"Could I go and get my cigarettes from the car please?" I asked.

"Mine too please!" chimed Josue.

"Alright, fine. We have a long wait anyways," said the officer as he opened the car to get our cigarettes.

We both had exactly one cigarette each left and smoked them at the same time. About the time we finished them, we heard the roar of thunder and felt the first droplets of rain.

Chapter 28: Black Hole Sun

The rain poured heavily over us. The state trooper went to his car and put on a poncho while Josue and I reminisced about the trip and it's twist ending, knowing that it may be the last time we see each other for a couple of days. We waited for an hour and a half in the rain until we saw another car with flashing lights pull up.

The car read *Sheriff of Mayes County*, and, sure enough, the sheriff stepped out of the car and in his hand, the leash to his pet K-9. The dog was off the clock yet they still bought him to speed things up as I kept insisting that the state trooper not search my car. I made eye contact with the sheriff hoping to garner some sympathy.

"Misdemeanors only," said the sheriff to the state trooper.

The sheriff began circling the car with the K-9 until the dog barked at the backseat where we had hidden the Jack Daniels. The trooper turned to us.

"Damn it! All I expected was honesty, now's your last chance to explain yourselves!" said the state trooper.

"Ok it's an empty bottle of Jack Daniels. That's it," I replied.

"Oh it's too late for apologizing. I have to search this car now," said the state trooper as he began with the driver's seat.

In the front left side, he found my one hitter and my bubbler. In the back left side, he found the bottle of Jack Daniels. In the back right side, he found two flasks which we used to store some of the whiskey. In the front left side, he found the weed, wax, another one hitter, and our dab vape pen. In addition, both Josue and I were under 21 at the time.

Altogether our crimes accounted to six misdemeanors and a felony. After the state trooper closed the passenger seat's door, everything hit me. I knew what I had to do. I looked at Josue with a sorry look on my face. I handed him my credit card and some cash. The state trooper walked towards us.

"Alright who's first?" said the state trooper as he unhooked his handcuffs from his waist.

I reached for my wallet as I stood up and threw my credit card in Josue's direction. He looked confused.

"All of it is mine," I said.

"You have the right to remain silent. Anything you say can and will be used against you in a court of law. You have the right to an attorney. If you cannot afford an attorney, one will be provided for you. Do you understand the rights I have just read to you? With these rights in mind, do you wish to speak to me?" said the state trooper as he cuffed me.

The officer put me in the front seat of the car and got in from the other side.

"Are you sure all of it is yours?" he asked while Josue was still confused by what I did.

"Yes sir. All of it. I have a bank history to prove it. Let Josue take the car and go," I said.

The state trooper angrily tossed my car keys in Josue's direction and left him with all the information about my arrest. As I sat in the cop car waiting for the state trooper to come back, I began messing with his radio and turned up his volume. The song Black Hole Sun by Soundgarden came on as the State Trooper returned to turn the volume down. A couple of minutes later, we were off to the prison.

Chapter 29: Aftermath

We approached the prison from the main entrance. I waited at the reception table for a couple of minutes while the state trooper filled out all his paperwork. Soon after, the prison guards took my mugshots and scanned my fingerprints. After that, they handed me a torn white t-shirt and orange sweatpants. They put me in cell block A-6 with the only prisoners they could trust with me. This cell block was also one of the few cell blocks visible by the security guards. The cell had worn out brick walls and a white metal door with bulletproof glass and a mail slot. There was also an emergency button but it didn't work at all.

The doors opened up for dinner a couple of hours after my arrival. The main area had a TV and lunch tables for the inmates. I went out to call my girlfriend, the only number I could remember, and told her to let my family know what happened. After that I grabbed my tray off food and offered it to my cellmates. Happy with the transaction, they offered me protection from Friday until Monday. After three hours, we were locked back up in the cell blocks.

Apart from food breaks, the prison held 28 hour lockdowns every alternate day. During one of these lockdowns, my cell mate kept me fed with blueberry cakes and corn chips. They even taught me how to play spades. I was very fortunate to have those prisoners as cell mates.

In my spare time I meditated, prayed to every god I could think of, and even read the first half of the New Testament. During one of the food breaks I met another Indian, or, I should say, the only other Indian, and prayed with him for a while.

"None of us want to see you back here. So when you get out, stay out," said the Indian. All my cellmates nodded in unison.

After forty hours had passed, I received news that my bail had been set. The day was Saturday. Hoping Josue was still around, I began waiting for someone to come and take me out of the cell. Soon enough, I was taken out the cell and back to the lobby. They gave me back my belongings and I walked into the visitor's entrance to meet my bondsman. We walked towards his shop where I could see someone yelling my name.

Thinking it was Josue I began to walk ahead of my bondsman. As I got closer to the mystery man, it became very clear to me that it wasn't Josue. It turned out to be my father.

A tear rolled down my eye when I reached him. Behind him my aunt and uncle walked out of the bondsman's shop. Up until that moment I had never known what true guilt felt like. But in that moment I felt so sorry for the crimes I had committed.

"I'm just glad you're ok," said my dad holding back his tears.

After doing some paperwork with the bondsman, I was informed that my initial court date was set on Monday. We drove to Arkansas to spend the night before driving to Oklahoma the next day. The first thing I wanted to do was take a bath.

I found myself holding my head underwater just yelling the entirety of my bath. I didn't want to step out. Ashamed of myself, I waited for everyone to finish eating before I ate my dinner. Traumatized by the long lockdowns, my dad gave me his watch to ease my anxiety. After dinner, I called Josue. He had Rocket Man playing on another phone's speaker held up to the microphone on his phone. He had to go back to work shortly after the song ended but it still stuck with me as a touching moment. Shortly after I hung up I fell asleep.

The next day my dad and I drove to Oklahoma to stay in a hotel near the court room. We stayed up most of the night ironing our suits, polishing our shoes, and shaving off our beards to look professional for the judge.

The next morning we woke up and drove to the court room where my lawyer was waiting for us. We stepped into the court room and checked in. While in the court room, I noticed one of cell mates sitting in front of the judge. We waved at each other. I was sitting in the back of the right column of benches nervously tapping my foot on the ground. I found that constantly looking at the time helped ease my new found anxiety. The judge walked in fifteen minutes after we entered.

The judge called out my name, read out only three misdemeanors, and scheduled my sentencing in August.

I was relieved! I was ecstatic at the fact that I wasn't a felon anymore, and thanked my lawyer a dozen times before we left the court room.

After the whole fiasco, my dad and I went out to grab one last bite before we flew back to Atlanta.

At the Arkansas airport I went to a candy shop to quench my thirst for a Twix bar. The cashier rung up my bar.

"Cash or credit?" asked the cashier.

"Credit please," I replied. I reached for my wallet but couldn't find my credit card. The cashier noticed that I couldn't find my card.

"Well you're S.O.L!" joked the cashier.

"What does that mean?" I asked.

"Sh*t out of luck," he replied.

"That's pretty funny. I'm going to steal that dude. Anyway, here's some cash. Keep the change," I said before walking back to my terminal.

We boarded the flight and I passed out whilst listening to the legendary Rocket Man.

We landed in Atlanta late at night and took an Uber home. After I said hi to my family, I hopped into the Prius and drove to meet Josue at Pizza Hut. He was just getting off work. Soon after we lit our cigarettes, it started pouring like crazy. I was still in my suit and he was in his work clothes. We sat under a gas station ceiling and talked about life. And when we decided it was time to leave Josue turned to me before stepping into his car.

"That was one hell of a ride," he said.

"It sure was."

Made in the
USA
Columbia, SC